better together*

*This book is best read together, grownup and kid.

 akidsco.com

a
kids
book
about

a kids book about TYPE 1 DIABETES

by Karli George

a
kids
book
about

A Kids Book About, Kids Are Ready, and the colophon
'a' are trademarks of A Kids Book About, Inc.

Printed in the United States of America.

A Kids Book About books are available online: *akidsco.com*

To share your stories, ask questions, or inquire about bulk
purchases (schools, libraries, and nonprofits), please use
the following email address: *hello@akidsco.com*

Print ISBN: 978-1-958825-13-6
Ebook ISBN: 978-1-958825-14-3

Designed by Rick DeLucco
Edited by Emma Wolf

For Scott: You showed me how to live this thing with grace.

For Sean & Andy: When the world said, "No," I said, "Yes."

And for Daryll: When counting my blessings, I count you twice.

Intro

The very word diabetes is enough to frighten even the bravest of souls. And I understand why—with type 1 diabetes, one needs insulin to stay alive, and this scares most people. But with management, life with diabetes can be full and rich, so it's really important to learn about it.

3 important facts I want you to know:

1) Ask anyone taking insulin shots how painful it is and they'll likely start smiling. It's NO BIGGIE. Most people will simply say, "It keeps me alive and well."

2) You did NOTHING wrong to get diabetes! You didn't eat too much sugar, and you weren't too lazy. Don't forget this truth, as it will never change.

3) You can live well with diabetes! Don't think you're only allowed to eat vegetables and boring stuff; that's not true! You'll learn to live in moderation and understand what keeps your body healthy—sometimes even more intuitively than people without diabetes!

A type 1 diabetes diagnosis is not a death sentence. Rather, it's an opportunity to live a full, happy, and healthy life. You'll be a role model. Strong. Brave. Get ready to become a superhero!

Hi.

My name's Karli.

And I have type 1 diabetes.

There are 2 kinds of diabetes:

type 1 and type 2.

This book is about type 1
because that's what I know.

Type 1 diabetes is generally diagnosed before age 25, and people usually find out they have it when they're kids.

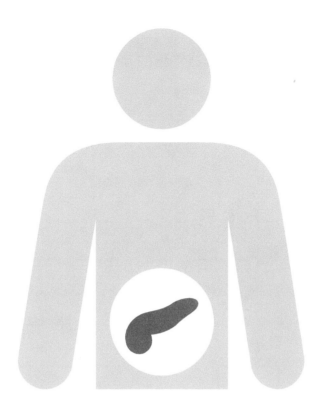

Type 1 diabetes involves the pancreas, which is an organ behind the stomach.

One of the main functions
of the pancreas is to release
the chemical insulin.

Insulin is responsible for carrying sugar out of the bloodstream to the billions of cells in your body.

Cells need nourishment, which is delivered by insulin.*

*Remember when I said there were 2 kinds of diabetes? Most people with type 2 diabetes create insulin, but their bodies resist it. And, historically, most people with type 2 diabetes were diagnosed in adulthood instead of as kids.

If someone has type 1 diabetes, their pancreas no longer creates insulin.

And without insulin, there's no way to get sugar out of the bloodstream, so it just keeps building up with nowhere to go.

Did you know that a normal
blood sugar is between about
70-100 mg/dL?*
*(miligrams per deciliter of blood)

When I was diagnosed with type 1 diabetes, my blood sugar was **1,496 mg/dL!** That's WAY too high.

Leading up to my diagnosis,
I was constantly thirsty.

One day, I drank over 2 gallons of
water (which is a lot) and still felt
like I couldn't get enough to drink.

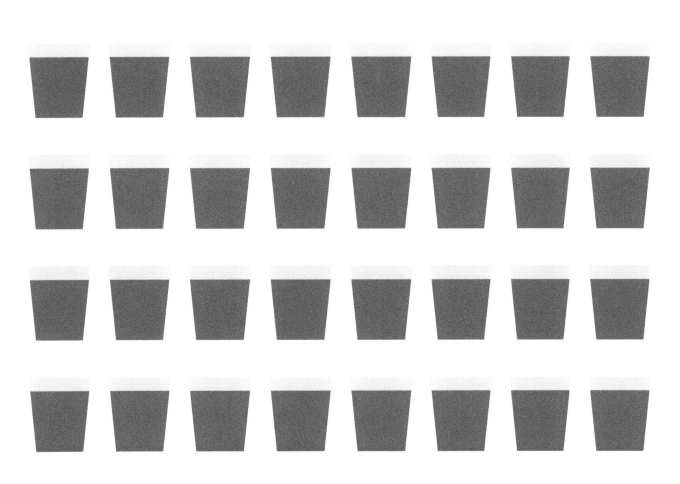

I was also going to the bathroom multiple times per hour, and all of the energy from the food I ate was turned into urine and immediately leaving my body.

Sometimes I was really hungry and ate as much as I could.

Sometimes I wasn't hungry at all.

Either way, I lost a lot of weight.

I was also almost blind by the time I was diagnosed.

These are common symptoms
for people with type 1 diabetes.

And I know that probably
sounds scary.

I was definitely scared as a kid,
thinking about living my life
with type 1 diabetes.

When the doctor told me how
high my blood sugar was,
he told me I was dying.

Without any intervention,
he said I would probably go blind,
I might lose a foot or a leg,
my kidneys might fail, and that
I shouldn't have a family of my own.

This was *so* sad to hear.

But do you want to hear something

awes

Today,
I have 2 sons,
5 granddaughters,
both of my feet,
my eyesight,
and working kidneys!

And now, I'm a nurse who
helps others who have diabetes.

All of this was possible because I made the decision early on to manage my diabetes and learn to live with it.

Finding the right balance
hasn't always been easy.

And it's normal to feel sad, angry,
and overwhelmed by it all.

Those feelings always come with big changes.

And to me, it was worth it to eventually come to terms with the changes and learn how to live my new reality— and you'll learn too!

First of all
(and with your doctor's help),
find the insulin option that is best for you.

That's right; you can replace the insulin your body is missing!

There are many choices and they all work much better now compared to when I was diagnosed.

The first insulin I used actually came from healthy pigs!

True story!

Today, insulin is much more pure, and it works better at lowering blood sugar and keeping it stable.

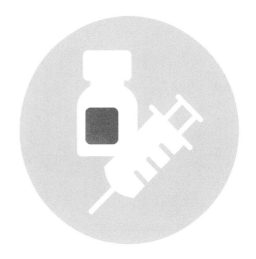

You can get insulin through a syringe and bottle, an insulin pen, a pump, and researchers are even developing an insulin nasal spray!

Whichever method is right for you,

they're all effective, and the one that's easiest for you is best because you'll use it for the rest of your life.

Insulin can be intimidating because it has to be injected.

It's a very fragile hormone, which is why you can't just swallow it.

But insulin keeps you alive and healthy!
And it's what will allow you to feel well
and do all the things you love.

Another important daily practice is testing your blood sugar.

And again, there are lots of devices to help with that!

You need to monitor your blood sugar at all times.

Everybody's diabetes is different and it's important to keep your blood sugar in a healthy range for you.

When your blood sugar gets to about 90 or lower, you can get what's called hypoglycemia (also called "crashing").

What that means is that your brain and cells aren't getting enough sugar.

You can experience many
different things, including:

- **Feeling shaky**

- **Cold sweats**

- **Hunger**

- **Extreme tiredness**

- **Darkened vision or seeing spots**

- **Indecisiveness**

- **Thinking unreasonably**

This can happen when
you miss a meal, are late for a meal,
or if you've done a lot of exercise
without having eaten in a while.

In my experience, the best way to safely get out of hypoglycemia is liquid sugar (about 5–8 ounces of soda or juice) or about 4 glucose tablets.

Oftentimes, hypoglycemia can happen in the middle of the night.

So check your blood sugar before bed and make sure you're at a safe level.

And it's always a good idea to keep glucose tablets close by so you can be ready if your sugar does get low!

This all probably
sounds overwhelming.

And I totally understand that.

The truth is, type 1 diabetes is about life and death.

We don't get to take a break from managing our diagnoses— it's an everyday thing.

But you *can* do everything you've always loved to do. Sometimes, it just takes some extra work and attention.

And before you know it, you'll be

an expert of

and what it

your body needs.

There will be bad days
from time to time, but each day
is a new opportunity to learn more
and keep growing.

Give yourself time,
and be kind to yourself, too.

Find a support group or role model
to encourage and remind you that
you aren't alone in this journey.

I read a lot of stuff about diabetes that sounds scary, like it's the #1 cause of blindness and amputations.

But I want to reframe how we think about type 1 diabetes, because I believe it's also the #1 cause of:

fortitude.
strength, courage.
empathy.
compassion.
capacity, capability.
body awareness.
maturity, grit,
and bravery.

Important Terms

A1C: The lab test that measures a person's average blood sugar over a 2-to-3 month period of time.

Autoimmune: A disorder in which the immune system mistakenly attacks and destroys tissue it believes is foreign.

Basal: A steady trickle of longer-acting insulin, such as that used in insulin pumps.

Bolus: An extra amount of insulin to cover an expected rise in blood glucose often related to a meal.

Blood Glucose Monitor: A small, portable meter used to determine how much sugar is in the blood which requires a blood sample to perform.

Continuous Glucose Monitor (CGM): A device that measures glucose levels automatically throughout the day in real time and is worn outside the body on an arm or abdomen, requiring no blood sample.

Dawn Phenomenon: The early morning (4-8:00 am) rise in blood sugar level that everyone has which may stay higher later in the morning for diabetics.

Honeymoon phase: A brief period of time (weeks or months) when someone diagnosed with type I diabetes will continue to secrete small amounts of insulin, rendering the blood sugar normal or near normal once insulin injections are initiated.

Hypoglycemia: When the sugar level in the blood is lower than target, usually less than 70 mg/dl, often referred to as "crashing."

Hyperglycemia: Elevated blood sugar indicative of diabetes.

Insulin: A hormone that helps the body use glucose for energy.

Insulin pen: A device for injecting insulin that holds disposable cartridges of insulin.

Insulin pump: An insulin delivery device worn outside the body which includes a tiny plastic catheter inserted just under the skin. Users will set the basal rate for a slow trickle of insulin continuously throughout the day and release a bolus insulin at meals or to correct for high blood sugar.

Ketone: A chemical produced when there is not enough insulin, resulting in the liver having to break down fat for energy.

Ketoacidosis (or Diabetic Ketoacidosis): A dangerous ketone build-up in the blood and urine when insulin levels are too low which causes nausea, vomiting, and stomach pain.

Lipodystrophy: Loss of fat under the skin resulting in small dents, usually caused by repeated shots of insulin in the same area.

Sliding Scale: A set of instructions for adjusting short-acting insulin on the basis of blood sugar levels using fast-acting insulin.

Outro

I have 2 objectives for this book. First, understand that diabetes is a serious matter and can't be ignored. We all need insulin if we want to live. These shots are our friend, not our enemy! They keep us feeling well. They keep us alive!

Second, and just as important, you can 100% do this! You will learn how strong, capable, and brave you are. When we were 12, my cousin Scott was diagnosed with type I diabetes. I remember thinking, "If I got diabetes, I would die. I could never give myself a shot!" Scott did it with ease. He wasn't afraid. He just did it.

And then, I got it too. I thought of Scott first. If he can do it, so can I! I think people with diabetes are strong. Good problem solvers. More aware. Persistent. Hard-working. Disciplined. Motivated. Empathetic. And you will be too. Now, go out and change the world.

About The Author

Karli George (she/her) is a bona fide, full-blooded Oregonian who loves all things fall, dark rainy days, vintage architecture, and celebrating Christmas year-round. It is not unusual for her to be listening to holiday music in March or burning an autumn harvest candle in late July.

Karli graduated from nursing school with the goal of helping people manage their diabetes in an empathetic and realistic way. If she could have 1 wish it would be for everyone with diabetes to have the confidence to make good decisions early on, believe that they have the power to overcome adversity, and have the opportunity to gain attributes they may not obtain otherwise. Reaching her 5th decade with diabetes has taught her that a life chock-full of shenanigans, hijinks and tomfoolery is definitely the way to go!

f Diabetes-in-the-real-with-Karli-CDCES

kids
book
about
BEING
INCLUSIVE

by Ashton Mota
& Rebekah Bruesehoff

kids
book
about
diversity

kids
book
about
LEADer
SHIP

by Orion Jean

a
kids
book
about
SAFETY

by Soraya Sutherlin, CEM
in partnership with JUBY

a
kids
book
about
CLIMATE
CHANGE

by Zanagee Artis
& Olivia Greenspan

a
kids
book
about
IMAGINATION

by LEVAR BURTON

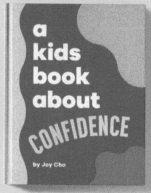

a
kids
book
about
CONFIDENCE

by Joy Cho

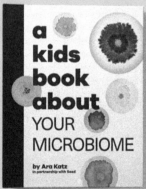

a
kids
book
about
YOUR
MICROBIOME

by Ara Katz
in partnership with Seed

a
kids
book
about
racism

by Jelani Memory

a
kids
book
about
DISABILITIES

by Kristine Napper

a
kids
book
about
DIVORCE

by Ashley Simpo

a
kids
book
about
cancer

by Dr. Kelsie Storm & Sarah Porter

a
kids
book
about
BEING
TRANSGENDER

by Gia Parr
in partnership with The GenderCool Project

a
kids
book
about
DEPRESSION

by Kileah McIlvain

a
kids
book
about
THE TULSA

Printed in the USA
CPSIA information can be obtained
at www.ICGtesting.com
LVHW061254250923
759185LV00015B/855